Mystery on the Island

Written by
Rob Waring and **Maurice Jamall**

Before You Read

to be sick

to sing a song

to take a picture

beach

camera

coat

forest

island

marina

pop music

secret

sound

video

In the story

Daniela

David

John

Faye

Tyler

woman

"Let's go in here," says Daniela. "Come on."
Daniela, David and John are walking in Bayview.
It is a great day in Bayview. It is Saturday morning
and everybody is shopping. The friends are going
to the music store. They want to buy some CDs.

A big white car is going very fast. It nearly hits Daniela.
"Wow! That car nearly hit me!" says Daniela.
"Yes, I know. Are you okay, Daniela?" asks John.
She says, "Yes, I think so. Why's that car going so fast?
Where's it going?"
"I don't know," says David, "But, maybe it's going to
Bayview Marina, over there."

Later, when they are walking near the marina, David sees the car again.

"There's that car! It's near that big boat. Can you see it?" asks David.

John says, "Yes, I can."

"What are the men doing?" asks Daniela.

"I don't know. But I don't like it," answers David.

"Let's go and see," John says.

They go to the car. They watch the men. They are
big and strong. A man takes a woman out of the
car. He takes her to the boat.

"Where's he taking that woman?" asks Daniela.

David says, "I think he's taking her onto the boat."

A man comes to them. "Go away," he says. He is big and angry.

"Who's that woman?" asks David.

"Go away!" says the man again. "Go away!"

Everybody is very surprised and they walk away. The man goes back to the boat.

"Why's that man so angry? Why doesn't he want us to see the woman?" asks Daniela. "I don't like this. I think that woman is in trouble," says Daniela. "Let's tell the police."

They all go to the police station.
Daniela talks to the police officer. She tells him about the car and the boat.
"Some men put a woman on a boat. We think they are taking her somewhere!" she says.
"I see," says the police officer. "Did you write down the car's number?" he asks.
"Umm . . . No," says David. "We didn't."
The police officer asks, "What was the name of the boat?"
"I didn't see it," says John.

"But they took the woman on to the boat," says David.
"We think she's in big trouble," says Daniela.
David asks, "Please come and look."
"Okay, let's go," says the police officer. "Where's the boat?"
he asks.
"It's down at the marina," they say. "Please be quick!"
They all go to the marina in the police car.

But the boat is not there. The men and the big white car are not there. And the woman is not there.

"Where are they?" asks the police officer.

David says, "They're not here."

"Then I can't help you," says the police officer. "I think you're making trouble!"

"But the woman was here!" says Daniela.

"There's no boat and no woman here, now," says the police officer. "Don't make trouble!"

John, Daniela and David are angry with the police officer.
They tell their friends, Faye and Tyler, about the woman.
"There was a man. And there was a woman in a long red
coat. The man put her on a big boat," says Daniela.
"Where are the boat and woman, now?" asks Faye.
David says, "We don't know!"
"Let's go down to the marina and look for the boat.
Maybe it will come back," says Faye.

Later, they all go down to the marina. They see the big boat and the police officer. He is talking to the man from the boat. He is smiling.

"Look!" says John. "That's the police officer. He's talking to the man."

"Maybe the woman is okay," says David.

The big boat leaves. Daniela goes to the police officer. She talks to him.

"Is the woman okay?" asks Daniela.

"What woman?" asks the police officer.

John says, "The woman on the boat."

"What boat?" says the police officer. "Sorry, I don't know anything about a boat. I don't know anything about a woman. Now go away." They are all very surprised and they walk away.

"I don't understand. That's very strange," says Daniela.
"Yes," says David. "He knows about the boat. And he was with the man from the boat. Then he says he doesn't know about the boat. Something's wrong!"
John says, "He's not telling us something."
"Why?" asks Faye. "Why's the police officer telling a lie?"
"Let's find out," says Tyler.
"Look, there's the boat," says John. "It's going to Shark Island. Quick. Let's go and look."

"How can we get there?" asks John.
"Let's go in *our* boat," says Daniela. "We must find her. We must help her."
They all get into their small boat. They follow the big boat to Shark Island.
"It's stopping over there," says Faye. "Let's go to another beach. I don't want them to see us," she says.
"Great idea," says Tyler. He takes the boat to a small beach.

On the beach, they hear something. "What's that sound?" asks John. "Can you hear it?"

"Yes, what is it?" asks Daniela. "Listen. The sound's coming from over there."

"But nobody lives on this island," says Faye.

Soon, they hear the sound again. "What's that sound?" John asks.

"Let's go and see," says Daniela. "This way," she says.

They walk through the forest. They do not want anybody to see them. They are following the sound. They are all very excited. Suddenly, Faye sees a big house.

"Look, there's a big old house," says Faye. "The sound may be coming from there. The woman may be there, too," she says.

"But nobody lives in that house," says Daniela. "It looks too old."

They go nearer the house. "No," says John. "There are some men and their dogs, can you see them?"

"Look! It's the man from the marina!" Faye says.

"What are they doing?" asks John.

"I don't know," says Tyler. "Let's go and see," he says.

"No, it's too dangerous. I don't like this place," says Daniela. "The men look big and strong and there are many big dogs. I don't care. I'm scared. I'm going home."

Suddenly, the man sees them. "What are *you* doing here?" he asks angrily.

David shows the man his camera. "We were taking pictures and we heard a big sound."

"No pictures! Come with us," the man says angrily.

Faye wants to know about the sound. "What was that sound?" she asks.

"Where are we going?" says Tyler. "Who are you?"

"Don't ask!" says the man. He takes them to the big house.

"Look! There's the woman from the boat!" says Daniela. "She *is* here!"

Tyler says, "Wow! It's Patti Sanders, the pop singer!"

"Patti Sanders!" says Daniela. "I love her music! I sing her songs all the time! What's she doing here?" she asks the man.

The man says, "She's making a music video."

"Oh, I see! So the sound was her music!" says Daniela.

"Yes, that's right," says the man. "We want to make the video, but we don't want people here. It's too much trouble," he says. "We want it to be a secret."

"Look, there's the police officer!" says John.

Faye says, "So the police officer knows you're here, too. He knows you're making a secret video!"

"Yes, that's right! He's helping us," says the man. "Do you want to meet Patti?" he asks.

"Of course!!" says Daniela.

"Hello, I'm Patti," she says.

Daniela says, "Hello, I'm Daniela. I'm very happy to meet you. I know all your songs. I love them."

"Thank you," says Patti.

Daniela is so excited. "I love singing your songs," she says.

"Yes, she's a good singer," says Faye.

"Yes, very very good," says John. "She sings your songs all the time."

"Really?" says Patti. "One of my singers is sick. She can't sing today."

"Oh, no," says Daniela. "And I wanted to watch you sing."

Patti asks, "Daniela, do you know my new song *Shining Star*?"

"Yes," replies Daniela. "I sing it all the time."

"I need somebody to help me. Do you want to sing it with me?" asks Patti.

"Now? Here? On video? Oh, yes please! Yes, please! Yes, please!!" shouts Daniela. She is very excited.

Daniela is singing with Patti up on stage. Her friends are sitting watching them.

"*You're my shining star . . .*," sings Daniela.

Patti is smiling at Daniela. Everybody is watching them sing.

"Daniela's a good singer," says Faye.

"Yes, very good," says John. "And today she's a star, too."